D0494969

H46 325 832 7

STEP-UP
HISTORY

Why did Henry VIII marry six times?

John Gorman

Evans

Published by Evans Brothers Limited
2A Portman Mansions
Chiltern Street
London W1U 6NR

Reprinted 2007, 2008

Produced for Evans Brothers Limited by
White-Thomson Publishing Ltd,
Bridgewater Business Centre,
210 High Street,
Lewes, East Sussex BN7 2NH

Printed in Hong Kong by New Era Printing Co. Ltd.

Project manager: Ruth Nason

Designer: Helen Nelson, Jet the Dog

Consultant: Rosie-Turner Bisset, Reader in
Education and Director of Learning and Teaching,
Faculty of Education, University of Middlesex.

The right of John Gorman to be identified as the
author of this work has been asserted by him in
accordance with the Copyright, Designs and
Patents Act 1988.

All rights reserved. No part of this publication
may be reproduced, stored in a retrieval system
or transmitted in any form, or by any means,
electronic, mechanical, photocopying, recording
or otherwise, without the prior permission of
Evans Brothers Limited.

Website addresses included in this book were
valid at the time of going to press. The Publishers
cannot take responsibility for later changes in
location or content.

British Library Cataloguing in Publication Data

Gorman, John

Why did Henry VIII marry six times?- (Step-up
history)
1. Henry, VIII, King of England, 1491-1547 -
Juvenile literature
2. Great Britain - Kings and rulers - Juvenile
literature
3. Great Britain - History - Henry VIII, 1509-
1547
I. Title
942'.052'092

ISBN 978 0 237 53040 2

Picture acknowledgements:

Ancient Art and Architecture Collection: page 8b
(N. Wilson); Art Archive: page 14 (Magdalene
College Cambridge/Eileen Tweedy); Bridgeman Art
Library: pages 1 and 15 (Harrogate Museums and
Art Gallery), 5 (Centrale Bibliotheek van de
Universiteit, Ghent, Belgium), 6l and 8t (The Berger
Collection at the Denver Art Museum, USA), 7l and
18r (Hever Castle Ltd, Kent), 10 (Chateau de
Versailles, France; Lauros/Giraudon), 11b (British
Library, London), 13b (Private Collection), 16
(Private Collection), 26 (© National Museum and
Gallery of Wales, Cardiff), 27 (Private Collection);
Corbis: pages 12 (Franz-Marc Frei), 19 (Jonathan
Blair), 24 (Jonathan Blair); Mary Evans Picture
Library: pages 13t, 20, 25l; Michael Nason: page
17; The Royal Collection © 2005, Her Majesty
Queen Elizabeth II: page 21; Topfoto.co.uk: cover
(main and top right) and pages 4, 6r, 7cl, 7cr
(Collection Roger-Viollet), 7r (Collection Roger-
Viollet), 9, 11t, 18l (HIP/Ann Ronan Picture Library),
23, 25r. © Evans Brothers Limited 2006

Maps and drawings by Helen Nelson.

Contents

The Tudor dynasty

Henry VIII became King of England in 1509, when he was 18. Find him on this family tree of the Tudor royal family.

The Tudors ruled England from 1485 to 1603.

◄ *The first Tudor monarch was Henry VII. This is the marriage medal of Henry VII and Elizabeth of York. Their marriage brought together two families who had been on opposite sides in the Wars of the Roses.*

Henry VII   m.   Elizabeth of York
(reigned 1485-1509)

Arthur m. Catherine of Aragon	Margaret	Mary
(died 1502)		

Henry VIII   m.   Catherine of Aragon   Anne Boleyn   Jane Seymour   Anne of Cleves   Catherine Howard   Catherine Parr
(reigned 1509-47)   (divorced 1533)   (beheaded 1536)   (died 1537)   (divorced 1540)   (beheaded 1542)   (died 1548)

Mary I   Elizabeth I   Edward VI
(reigned   (reigned   (reigned
1553-58)   1558-1603)   1547-53)

Henry VII, the first Tudor king

Henry VII became king after winning a battle against Richard III. This was the last battle of the Wars of the Roses, which took place in England from 1455 to 1485, between two sides who claimed the crown of England.

Henry VII was a strong and determined ruler who wanted to make England wealthier and more powerful. One way of doing this was to encourage trade with other countries. Another way was to avoid going to war, as this was very expensive.

In the 30 years of the Wars of the Roses it was often unsafe for people to go out. Many people believed that a strong king was needed to keep England safe and peaceful in future.

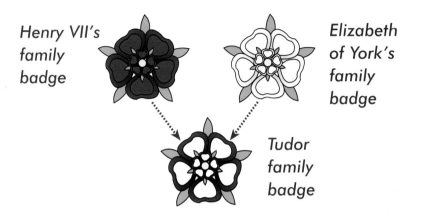

Henry VII's family badge

Elizabeth of York's family badge

Tudor family badge

After Henry VII married Elizabeth of York, a new family badge showing both roses became the Tudor symbol.

To prevent war, Henry tried to make alliances with the royal families of other countries. He arranged for his children to marry members of these families. For example, his eldest son, Arthur, was married to a Spanish princess, Catherine of Aragon.

The heir to the throne

Arthur was the eldest son of Henry VII and so he was the heir to the throne: he would be the next king. However, Arthur died in 1502 and Henry, then aged 10, became the heir.

His father, Henry VII, arranged that Henry would be married to Catherine of Aragon (Arthur's widow) when he was old enough. He supervised his young son closely and gave him little freedom. He chose Henry's companions and activities.

Ambassadors wrote that, at age 17, Henry spent most of his time in a room next to the king's bedchamber. A year later Henry VII died and Henry VIII was crowned king. At age 18, Henry was the richest, most powerful man in the kingdom.

Henry's marriages

Below is a timeline of Henry's marriages. Why do you think he married six times? Try making a list of some possible reasons and then, as you read more of this book, see how many of your possible reasons you find.

1 Catherine of Aragon

Henry's first marriage, to Catherine of Aragon, was the longest. They were happy together for many years but only one of their children, Mary, survived. Henry was determined to have a son, and so he divorced Catherine in 1533.

2 Anne Boleyn

Henry married Anne Boleyn in 1533 and Anne gave birth to a daughter, Elizabeth, in the same year. Only a few months after marrying Anne, Henry's feelings about her changed. When he met another lady he wanted to marry, he told his advisers to find a way of getting rid of Anne. She was beheaded in 1536.

3 Jane Seymour

Soon after Anne was beheaded, Henry married Jane Seymour. Within a year Jane gave birth to a son, Edward, and Henry was delighted. Then Jane died.

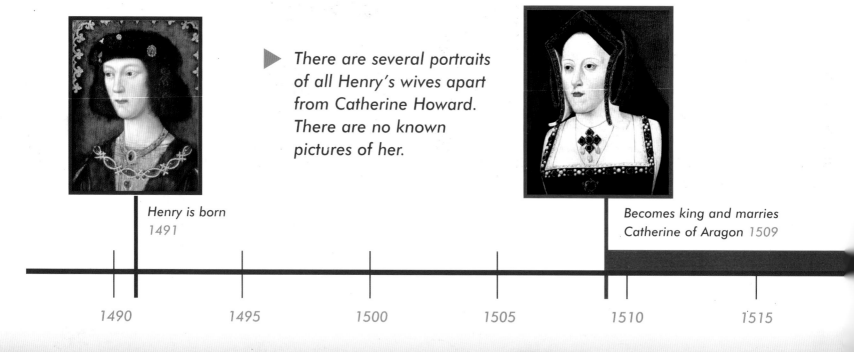

▶ There are several portraits of all Henry's wives apart from Catherine Howard. There are no known pictures of her.

Henry is born
1491

Becomes king and marries
Catherine of Aragon 1509

1490   *1495*   *1500*   *1505*   *1510*   *1515*

4 Anne of Cleves

In 1540 Henry married Anne of Cleves. This marriage was intended to strengthen links between England and German states. Henry agreed to marry Anne after seeing her portrait and reading reports about her. When they met, Henry found her unattractive. He divorced her within six months.

5 Catherine Howard

Catherine Howard was a cousin of Anne Boleyn. She was only 17 when Henry married her and he was thrilled with his pretty young wife. But when he found out that she had many boyfriends, he had her beheaded.

6 Catherine Parr

Henry married Catherine Parr in 1543. She became a companion and nurse to the king who was ill and in pain.

A rhyme to remember

Learn this rhyme about Henry's wives:

Divorced, Beheaded, Died, Divorced, Beheaded, Survived.

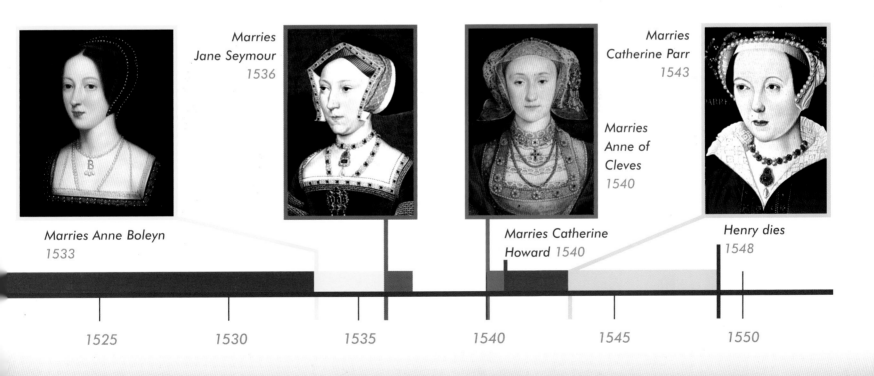

Marries Anne Boleyn
1533

Marries
Jane Seymour
1536

Marries Catherine
Howard 1540

Marries
Anne of
Cleves
1540

Marries
Catherine Parr
1543

Henry dies
1548

1525   1530   1535   1540   1545   1550

Portraits and paintings

Look carefully at these pictures of Henry. Portraits of the king show how his appearance changed from 1509, the year he was crowned, to later in his life. They also show how he wanted people to see him. Henry believed that a king should look grand and powerful, and this was quite easy for him as he was 194cm tall, broad-shouldered and muscular.

Paintings like these were displayed in Henry's palaces and so they were seen only by visiting ambassadors and members of Henry's court. But these were just the people that Henry wanted to impress. The ambassadors, from foreign countries, would tell their kings about him. The English nobles who made up his court would see his strength and not be tempted to plot against him.

▲ Make a list of the ways in which this portrait, painted in 1509, matches the description below, which was written in the same year.

▶ Henry was king of England, Wales and part of France. Two and a half million people were his subjects. The picture most of them would see of Henry was on coins.

His complexion fair and bright, with auburn hair and short in the French fashion, and a round face so beautiful that it would become a pretty woman, his throat being rather long and thick.

◀ *Which features of this portrait by Henry's court painter, Hans Holbein, make Henry look (a) wealthy and (b) masculine and powerful? The portrait measures 220 x 150 cm.*

Describe Henry

Imagine you are a foreign ambassador just arrived at the court of Henry VIII. You have not met the king yet, but you have seen the new portrait by Hans Holbein. Write a letter to your own king, describing Henry's appearance, expression, pose and clothing.

Henry in old age

At the end of his life, according to one description, 'the king could not go upstairs unless he was let up and down by a device'. Do you think Henry would have allowed an artist to paint a full-length picture of him in his old age?

Henry and the court

In Tudor times the monarch made all the important decisions about governing the country. Henry was clever, but he needed advisers to help him with such a difficult task. These people lived and worked in the king's palace and were known as the court. The palace became a centre of government as well as a home.

▼ *In 1520 Henry went to meet the king of France, to try to arrange an alliance. Both kings took their court with them and wanted to impress each other. Tents covered with golden cloth were put up for banquets and entertainment.*

Fifty-four palaces

In fact, by the end of his reign, Henry had 54 palaces spread throughout the country. In winter the court stayed near London, usually at Greenwich Palace. In summer it moved around to other palaces. This meant that the king was seen by more of his subjects. Also it was safer to be out of London in the summer, as diseases spread rapidly there in the warmer months.

The brilliance and richness of Henry's palaces impressed visitors, as Henry hoped. Ambassadors who visited wrote letters

Henry's largest palace was at Hampton Court, near London.

describing the fine tapestries, Turkish carpets, clocks and other luxuries in the royal chambers.

Banquets

Henry entertained his visitors with long, lavish banquets with up to ten courses. One visitor was amazed at all the types of meat offered to the court in one day in 1532:

> 6 oxen, 8 calves, 40 sheep, 12 pigs, 132 capons, 7 swans, 20 storks, 34 pheasants, 92 partridges, 192 cocks, 56 herons, 84 pullets, 720 larks, 240 pigeons, 24 peacocks and 192 plovers.

Which of these birds and animals do we still eat and which are rarely or never eaten today?

Entertainment

In the first half of his reign Henry put on pageants, dances, plays and music recitals to entertain the court. As he grew old and disabled there were fewer organised festivities, but making music, playing cards and, probably, gossip remained popular pastimes.

Tudor music

Visit http://sca.uwaterloo.ca/~praetzel/ TOD_2/ to hear some Tudor music played on Tudor instruments. 'Horses Bransle' is a good example of a tune using recorders. Imagine richly dressed people moving in time to it.

Which musical instrument is Henry playing in this picture?

Henry's pastimes

Henry VIII was energetic and loved sport. His favourite pastimes were hunting and jousting.

Hunting

The king hunted deer in the royal parks and forests on most days of the hunting season, from May to October. In summer the hunts lasted from dusk to dawn, leaving Henry little time for work. He rode his horses so fast that it was difficult for his companions to keep up with him. A courtier wrote that the king never hunted without tiring eight to ten horses.

Jousting

Jousting was a dangerous sport. Two mounted knights in armour charged at each other on either side of a barrier. They used their lances (long pointed spears) to try to knock each other off their horses. Imagine the skill needed to control the charging horse, aim the lance and dodge the opponent's weapon!

▼ *People went to watch jousting tournaments between teams of knights. You may be able to go to a re-enactment of one, like this.*

When jousting in 1524 Henry forgot to pull down the visor on his helmet. An onlooker wrote:

The people, seeing the king's face bare, cried hold, hold – Alas what a sorrow was it to the people when they saw the duke's lance strike the king's headpiece.

Henry recovered that afternoon, but ten years later, at another joust, he was trapped underneath his horse after a fall. He was unconscious for two hours and gave up jousting after this serious accident.

Other sports

It was said that, as a young man, the king could:

- defeat all comers fencing with the heavy two-handed sword;
- wrestle any man to the floor;
- draw a bow with greater strength than any man in England.

Not all of his pastimes were as active. As he grew older he took to hawking and bowling. Sometimes he was satisfied to be a spectator at bear-baiting and cockfighting contests.

Try your jousting skills

Visit http://www.tudorbritain.org and click on 'Jousting' to try your jousting skills.

◄ *The longbow was a weapon used in wars. The sports that Henry enjoyed also prepared him to lead his army.*

▶ *Another sport that Henry enjoyed was called 'real tennis'.*

Henry's problems

By the 1520s Henry VIII had some difficult problems to solve.

Shortage of money

It was very expensive to run the court, build palaces and raise armies. In addition, Henry had decided to expand England's navy. When he was crowned in 1509, the navy had eight ships. Henry built it up to 80 ships by 1545, so the cost was very great.

By the 1520s the tax that Henry collected did not cover all his expenses. He and his advisers needed to find an extra source of money. In 1523 Henry tried to charge a tax on property, but people threatened to revolt.

▲ Henry's flagship, the Mary Rose, was built in 1510. Which Mary in his family do you think he named the ship after? The Mary Rose was a powerful warship, used against France and against Scotland.

On board

Visit http://www.maryrose.org/lcity/ to find out more about the Mary Rose and try out all the jobs on board.

He had no son

Henry believed that England needed a king as its ruler. Therefore he needed a son to be his heir and he did not have one. His wife, Catherine of Aragon, had given birth six times, but only one of the children, Princess Mary, had survived.

Henry became more and more worried and said that God was stopping him having a son in order to punish him for marrying Catherine, who had been his brother's wife. Also Henry had fallen in love with Anne Boleyn, one of Catherine's ladies-in-waiting.

He wanted a divorce

Henry decided that he wanted to divorce Catherine, but there were difficulties:

- Catherine had been a good wife and would not accept divorce easily.
- She was a popular queen.
- Her nephew, Emperor Charles V, ruled over much of Europe. He was on her side.

- England was a Catholic country and Henry and Catherine had been married in a Catholic church ceremony. The marriage could not be ended without the permission of the Pope, the head of the Catholic Church.

Henry sent his chief adviser, Cardinal Wolsey, to seek the Pope's permission, but the Pope did not want to offend Emperor Charles V.

Efforts to make the Pope agree went on but in the end Henry lost patience. In January 1533, he secretly married Anne Boleyn. In May 1533 he got Archbishop Cranmer to declare that his marriage to Catherine had never been lawful.

An artist imagined the scene where Archbishop Cranmer told Catherine that her marriage to Henry was unlawful. King Henry looks on. What do you think Catherine is saying?

How Henry solved his money problem

New laws

In 1532 Henry ordered Parliament to meet and in the next four years they passed laws that freed the English Church from the Pope's control. In 1534 a law made the king the head of the Church in England. This gave the king control over ways of worship in England and also over all of the Church's possessions. These possessions included land, which amounted to one fifth of England and Wales.

Cromwell's plan

Much of the Church's land belonged to 600 monasteries spread throughout the country. King Henry's chief adviser was now Thomas Cromwell and he suggested that Henry should close the monasteries and sell the land.

Cromwell knew that his plan needed care, as the monasteries had been part of English life for centuries. People do not always like change. They knew that many of the monasteries provided help for the sick and the poor. The monasteries also gave people work, as servants and labourers.

▲ In Tudor times Parliament was made up of wealthy people from the nobility and gentry. Usually the monarch ruled without asking Parliament, but Henry knew that sometimes it was wise to have their agreement. This picture shows Henry and Parliament in 1523.

Investigating the monasteries

Cromwell needed to give reasons for closing the monasteries and so he sent teams of men to investigate. Then, in 1535, he claimed that they had found that the monks in the smaller monasteries were breaking the rules of the Church. Instead of living good, simple lives, they were leading lives of luxury.

Cromwell also said that, if the monasteries were closed and the king sold the land, he would never need to collect taxes again. Do you think Cromwell believed this?

Closing the monasteries

In 1536 the smaller monasteries were closed. There was little reaction in the south of England but in the north people rebelled. When 30,000 rebels gathered in York, outnumbering Henry's army, he agreed to re-open the monasteries. But in the spring, after the rebels had gone home, his army returned and executed 200 of the rebel leaders.

Next Henry closed the larger monasteries. He sold off their land quickly, at low prices, because he needed money urgently to pay his debts. He spent most of the money fighting wars against Scotland and France in the 1540s.

As for the abbot, we found ... that he delighted much in playing at dice and cards and therein spent much money ... it was confessed and proved that there was here such frequency of women coming to this monastery.

The number of monks was increasing, the prior was efficient, and the place flourished.

▲ ◀ How would Cromwell have used these two pieces of evidence to argue for closing the monasteries?

▼ After they were closed, many of the monastery buildings fell into ruin. Today they are cared for as historic sites for people to visit.

Religion in Tudor times

Visit http://www.tudorbritain.org and use the clues to see if people were free to choose their own religion in Tudor times.

Henry and Anne Boleyn

Henry first met Anne Boleyn in 1526, when she was one of Queen Catherine's ladies-in-waiting. One ambassador wrote that Anne looked quite plain apart from 'her eyes which are black and beautiful'. Anne had spent some time at the French court and perhaps it was there that she learned how to make men notice her and find her attractive.

Henry was attracted to Anne who was lively and intelligent. She understood Henry and knew how to get her own way.

Henry married Anne secretly in January 1533, but the marriage was not made lawful until May, after Henry's marriage to Catherine of Aragon had been judged unlawful.

This portrait of Henry was painted in about 1520, so he might have looked like this when he knew Anne Boleyn.

What did he send Anne with this love letter? Rex is Latin for king.

As I cannot be with you in person, I am sending you the nearest possible thing to that, namely, my picture set in a bracelet ...

Your loyal servant and friend

H Rex

The Latin writing in this portrait says 'Anne Boleyn, Queen of England, 1534'.

A. BOLEYN·REGINA ANGLIÆ·1534

Why did the marriage fail?

In September Anne gave birth to a daughter, Elizabeth. The doctors had predicted that she would have a son. Henry was too disappointed to attend the christening.

As time passed he realised that Anne was not the sort of wife he wanted. She argued with him and was quick to grumble. When she did not have another baby, Henry began to say that the marriage was 'cursed' – in other words, an evil spell had been cast over it. He said that he had been 'bewitched' by Anne. His words made it sound as though he saw her as a witch. This was a serious accusation to make, because in those days witches were executed. Henry also had a new wife in mind, Jane Seymour.

The Tower of London

Two of Henry's wives, Anne Boleyn and Catherine Howard, and other people who displeased the king were executed at the Tower of London. Take a tour of the Tower with Rascal Raven at http://www.towerof londontour.com/kids and then complete the quiz on the site.

Anne is beheaded

In April 1536 Henry ordered Cromwell to find a reason why his marriage to Anne could be ended. Cromwell could find no reason to end the marriage and so he made up accusations against Anne. He accused her, amongst other things, of plotting to take King Henry's life. Anne was put on trial and found guilty. She was executed in May 1536 at the Tower of London. Anne had not been a popular queen but no one believed her guilty.

▲ A guide at the Tower of London shows visitors where Anne was beheaded by sword on Tower Green.

Henry and Jane Seymour

Jane Seymour was one of Anne Boleyn's ladies-in-waiting. She knew that Henry was attracted to her when he sent her a purse of gold coins. Jane's family wanted her to encourage the king's friendship. They thought that, if Jane became queen, then her brothers, who were courtiers, would be given the most powerful jobs at court. Jane agreed to meet the king in secret and before long she promised to marry him.

The marriage took place in May 1536, ten days after Anne Boleyn was beheaded.

Henry's temper

Jane had been a courtier long enough to know Henry's ways. It was dangerous to argue with him, for he always thought that he was right. His temper terrified the court. He used to hit Cromwell, his chief adviser, around the head. However, Jane was calm and mild and she soothed and relaxed the king.

Only once, Jane interfered in Henry's affairs, when she pleaded with him not to kill some prisoners. He reminded her sharply of what happened to Anne Boleyn. Mostly, Jane spent her time walking her white poodle in the palace gardens, following the hunt or doing needlework with her ladies-in-waiting.

Thomas Cromwell was Henry's chief adviser in the 1530s. Make a list of things he did, from the information on pages 16-23. Many nobles in Parliament did not like Cromwell and tried to turn the king against him. In 1540, Cromwell was accused and found guilty of treason *and was executed at the Tower of London.*

A son is born

Henry had married Jane hoping to have a son. When she became pregnant in 1537 Henry was pleased. After she gave birth to a son, Henry cried with joy. The Tudor royal family had a male heir at last. He was named Edward. A writer described London on the day after his birth: 'church bells pealed out, bonfires were lit, free wine was handed out and there were street parties and banquets.'

News!

Write a newspaper article for the day of Edward's birth. Look at modern newspapers to find ideas for headlines and subheadings.

This painting shows Henry and Jane, with their son Edward, and Henry's daughters, Mary (left) and Elizabeth (right). How do we know this was painted some years after Jane's death?

Jane dies

Within a few days of Edward's birth Jane developed a fever and died. Henry was upset and wore dark mourning clothes for three months. He always spoke of Jane with affection and he was buried with her, at Windsor Castle, when he died.

A fortnight after Jane's burial Cromwell started the search for King Henry's next wife. Having one prince, Edward, was not enough, for in Tudor times many children died.

Henry and Anne of Cleves

Searching for an ally

Henry and his advisers wanted the king's next marriage to be with a foreign princess because they thought that England needed an ally in Europe. So Henry's ambassadors searched the European courts for suitable brides. It was not easy as Henry had a bad reputation as a husband. Also he was 48 and overweight, but wanted his wife to be young and attractive.

Cromwell suggested asking the Duke of Cleves, who had two unmarried sisters. As the ruler of Cleves, the Duke had made alliances with other German states which had broken away from the Pope's control. Cromwell thought that a marriage between Henry and one of the Cleves sisters would give England allies who were on the same side of the Catholic-Protestant division.

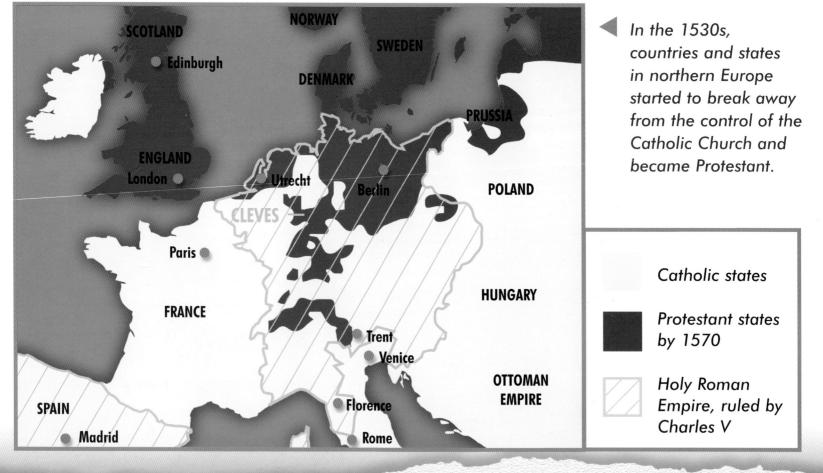

In the 1530s, countries and states in northern Europe started to break away from the control of the Catholic Church and became Protestant.

Catholic states

Protestant states by 1570

Holy Roman Empire, ruled by Charles V

Wealthy and working

Cut out the head and neck from two photos of yourself and paste them on to a large sheet of paper. Research Tudor costume in order to make one portrait of yourself as a wealthy Tudor and one as a working person in Tudor times.

◄ *This is the portrait that Henry's court artist, Hans Holbein, made of Anne of Cleves.*

Henry chooses

Henry had never met the sisters and so he sent his court artist, Hans Holbein, to paint them. After inspecting the portraits and reading his ambassador's reports Henry chose Anne.

The arrangements for the marriage went ahead and on 1 January 1540 Henry met Anne for the first time. He took an instant dislike to her. He told Cromwell later that she 'was nothing fair and has very evil smells about her'.

Henry was polite to Anne but angry with Cromwell and the other advisers who had praised the princess. She was not suited to be the queen as she spoke very little English and had been brought up to believe that singing, dancing, playing musical instruments and hunting – the favourite pastimes at the English court – were not suitable for a lady.

The shortest marriage

Henry married Anne in January. Not to do so would have been an insult to her brother. But within a few days Cromwell found a reason to end the marriage. Anne had been engaged before and this engagement had never been broken off. In Tudor times this made Anne's marriage to Henry unlawful. Anne was shocked but accepted the money and houses, including Hever Castle, that Henry gave her. Henry said that he would call her his sister.

Catherine Howard and Catherine Parr

Catherine Howard was a niece of the Duke of Norfolk, an important courtier. She was also a cousin of Anne Boleyn. Henry VIII met her when she came to court, aged 15 or 16, in 1539. How old was Henry then?

Catherine had not been well educated. She could sing and dance better than she could read and write. But she was very attractive and the king fell in love with her. One observer wrote that Henry had never been so in love.

Two groups of courtiers

Some courtiers liked the changes that were happening in religion since Henry became Head of the Church in England. Others did not. The Duke of Norfolk and his supporters were Catholics, who did not want the changes. They encouraged the friendship between Catherine and Henry. They thought that if Catherine became queen, the Duke (her uncle) might be given a powerful job in which he could prevent change.

Henry gave Catherine many gifts of jewels and land and by July 1540 they were married.

But quite soon Catherine had a love affair with a courtier. The Duke of Norfolk's opponents found out about this and their leader, Archbishop Cranmer, told the king. Within days Catherine was found guilty and executed.

▼ Catherine was executed on Tower Green, within the walls of the Tower of London. On the evening before, she practised resting her head on the executioner's *block*.

Henry in his old age. What has changed since the portrait on page 9 was painted?

Catherine Parr was 31 when she married Henry VIII in 1543.

Henry's sixth marriage

Now Cranmer and his followers had the upper hand at court and they were pleased when Henry married again in July 1543. His new wife, Catherine Parr, supported Cranmer's views.

Henry had aged quickly and Catherine was as much a nurse as a wife to him. Her kind ways soothed Henry, who was in constant pain from leg sores and headaches. She was also a thoughtful stepmother to Henry's children, Mary, Elizabeth and Edward.

Catherine outlived Henry, who died in 1547. She married Thomas Seymour and died in childbirth in 1548.

Job description

Think about what you have learned about Henry's character, responsibilities and concerns as a Tudor king. Write an advert inviting people to apply for the job of King Henry's wife. What qualities will they need?

Six marriages and three children

One reason why Henry married six times was that he wanted sons to follow him as Tudor kings. In the end he had only one son and two daughters. Each one of the three ruled England for some time.

Edward VI

Prince Edward was the first of Henry's heirs to rule. He was crowned king in 1547. Edward was then only nine years old so a group of advisers led by his uncle, Edward Seymour, ruled for him.

King Edward was never strong and he died when he was fifteen. During his reign many changes were made to religion in England. Henry VIII had broken away from the Pope's control but kept Catholic prayers and services. Now laws were passed that made a complete break with Catholic ways of worship.

◄ This painting shows Henry VIII and the Tudors who reigned after him. Mary I is on the left with her husband Philip II of Spain. A verse written around the edge of the painting describes Henry as 'a valiant father', Edward as 'a virtuous son', Mary as 'a zealous daughter' and Elizabeth as having all the qualities of the others.

Mary I

Queen Mary came to the throne in 1553. She disagreed with the changes made to the Church in her brother's reign. Her brother's advisers had made it unlawful to be a Catholic. Now Mary made it unlawful not to be a Catholic. She had people burned at the stake for refusing to follow her beliefs.

Elizabeth I

Elizabeth was crowned queen in 1558 on Mary's death. Elizabeth tried to avoid wars and to calm the arguments over religion. She chose able and loyal advisers. Her navy defeated a huge Spanish fleet called the Armada and saved England from invasion. Some people believe that she was the most successful of the Tudor monarchs. She died childless in 1603.

This is your life

Think of guests who might take part in a 'This is your life' TV programme for Henry VIII. Then choose, prepare and practise parts for a class drama performance of the programme.

▲ These people were led to London to be put on trial for being Protestants. Which monarch do you think was on the throne?

Changing his mind

Henry VIII owned a gold chain inscribed 'Prefer to die than change my mind'. Do you think that Elizabeth's reign would have changed his mind about female heirs?

Thinking back

Henry married because:

- He had fallen in love.
- He wanted a son to follow him on the throne.
- He needed to make an alliance with another country, to make England stronger.

For each of Henry's marriages, which reason do you think was the main one? Try making a list of the reasons why the marriages ended.

Glossary

alliance — an agreement between countries to fight or work together. In Tudor times alliances were often based on marriages between members of ruling families.

ally — a person or country that has agreed to help another, especially in times of trouble.

ambassador — a person who is sent abroad to represent his or her country. Ambassadors also send information to their own government about the country they have been sent to.

archbishop — a senior bishop.

bear-baiting — a sport in which savage dogs were urged to attack a chained bear.

bedchamber — a room in palaces and large houses which held a bed and other furniture. It usually had smaller rooms leading from it for dressing and washing.

behead — put someone to death by chopping off their head with an axe or sword.

bewitched — very influenced by someone's charms.

block — a piece of wood or stone used as a support for chopping or beheading.

cardinal — a senior bishop in the Catholic Church.

Catholic — a Christian whose religious leader is the Pope, who lives in Rome.

chamber — an old-fashioned name for a room, often used when the room was large and used for a particular purpose.

christening — the naming of a person during the Christian ceremony of baptism.

cockfighting — a sport in which two cockerels were forced to fight each other until death.

court — the palace household of a king or queen and the servants and courtiers who live there.

courtier — a noble who attends court to advise the monarch and to take part in the life of the court.

cursed — harmed as a result of being under a curse.

divorce — to lawfully end a marriage.

emperor — male ruler of an empire, a group of countries under a single ruler.

engaged — promised, in a formal way, to become the husband or wife of someone.

execute — to put someone to death as a legal punishment.

fencing — the sport of fighting with swords. The most skilled fencer wins the contest by scoring more points.

flagship — the ship carrying the commander of a navy, who is called an admiral.

gentry — the group of people in society just below the nobility in importance; often smaller landowners.

hawking	a sport using birds of prey such as falcons or hawks to kill or capture other birds.
heir to the throne	a prince or princess who will be the next monarch.
knight	a mounted soldier from a noble family who is trained in fighting skills.
ladies-in-waiting	young women who act as friends and companions to a queen or princess.
monarch	the ruler of a country – a king, queen, emperor or empress.
monastery	a building in which monks live, work and pray. The monks live under strict religious rules such as taking part in worship several times each day.
mourning	a time of sadness when someone dies.
navy	a country's warships and sailors.
nobility	the most powerful group of people in the country, made up of nobles.
nobles	landowning and usually rich families who helped the monarch to run the country. They have titles such as 'lord', 'duke' or 'sir'.
pageant	a procession or parade to entertain people.
Parliament	in Tudor times, a council of nobles who met to advise the monarch and discuss and pass new laws.
Pope	the head of the Catholic Church, who lives in Rome.
pregnant	expecting a baby.

Protestant	a Christian who does not have the Pope as their leader.
real tennis	also known as royal tennis – a Tudor game which developed into modern lawn tennis.
rebel	to resist or fight against the monarch or government.
revolt	to take part in a planned action against the monarch or government, for example refusing to pay taxes or burning down government buildings.
stake	a post to which a person is tied before being burned alive.
subjects	people ruled over by a monarch.
tax	money collected by the monarch or government to pay for the running of the country.
tournament	a competition between knights who fought each other with different weapons of war.
treason	trying to overthrow the monarch, or being disloyal to him or her.
visor	the moveable part of a helmet made to protect the face.
Wars of the Roses	a series of wars between two families in England: the Yorks (whose badge was a white rose) and the Lancasters (whose badge was a red rose).
witch	someone supposed to have magical powers, often imagined to be able to harm others with spells and curses.

For teachers and parents

This book is designed to support and extend the learning objectives for Unit 7 of the QCA History Scheme of Work.

The Tudor Age is a period of history that exerts a strong attraction on the English imagination. It tends to be regarded as something of a golden age when England triumphed against the Armada, founded the basis of an empire and built on the ideas of the Renaissance in politics, religion and literature. It is hard to find any period outside of modern times that has so many resources available to help the History teacher: Tudor buildings to visit, portraits and paintings to view and learn from, and plays, letters and wills to read and investigate. The interactive pupil websites used in this book enrich the work undertaken in a unique way. Valuable primary source material can be found at http://englishhistory.net/tudor/primary.html and in the Resources section of http://www.tudorbritain.org/.

During this study of Henry VIII and his wives, children have the opportunity to

- Place events in their correct order.
- Learn about the main features of court life and the power of the Tudor monarch.
- Learn about the experiences of individuals in the past and reflect on them.
- Identify reasons for changes in religion and their consequences.
- Investigate a range of sources.
- Ask and answer questions.
- Recall, select and organise material and present it to a group.
- Use ICT to support their learning.

There are opportunities for cross-curricular work in art, design technology, religion and literacy.

SUGGESTED FURTHER ACTIVITIES

Pages 4 - 5 The Tudor dynasty
Outline the events leading to the Wars of the Roses and the Battle of Bosworth. Explain the significance of Henry's marriage to Elizabeth of York and the symbolism of the Tudor rose. Emphasise the rather tenuous nature of the Tudor claim to the throne. Discuss with the children how this influenced the attitude of the early Tudor monarchs to others who claimed the throne. Henry VIII took every opportunity to rid himself of rivals, usually by execution.

Ask questions about the family tree to establish children's understanding and to familiarise them with the different relationships.

Visit http://www.tudorbritain.org > resources > trade > Tudor map of Europe. Print and enlarge the map and ask the children to compare it with Europe today. Remind them that the Tudors ruled only England, Wales and Calais in 1485. Scotland and England were united in 1603, whilst the conquest of Ireland was completed in the same year.

Pages 6 - 7 Henry's marriages
Discuss with the children how people choose a partner and why they marry. Avoid suggesting that one method is superior to another. Some children may belong to groups that have marriages arranged by their parents. Differentiate between 'arranged' and 'forced' marriages.

The children could make a display with notes about the personal badges of Henry VIII and his wives. Visit http://www.hrp.org.uk and select Hampton Court Palace > education > teachers' resources. Print and enlarge the clear outlines of the badges. Use the information to explain the way in which the badges were designed. Excellent coloured images of all the Tudor badges are at http://tudorhistory.org.

As part of this study, children could make their own personal or family badge. They could also visit the V&A museum website: http://www.vam.ac.uk > Things To Do Online > More Things To Do Online and design a coat-of-arms.

Pages 8 - 9 Portraits and paintings
Extend the activities by studying a wider range of Tudor portraits and paintings. The National Portrait Gallery publishes a 32-page booklet called *Tudor Portraits* by Claire Gittings (ISBN 1-85514-341-0). It is full of suggestions and approaches that work well.

Photocopy suitable Tudor portraits and pictures and ask the children to research the names of all the clothes on show. They can mount, label and display the photocopies. The website http://tudorhistory.org has many suitable images.

Children could study in detail the More family portrait at the V&A Museum website, www.vam.ac.uk > Things To Do Online > More Things To Do Online.

Pages 10 - 11 Henry and the court
If possible, visit Hampton Court Palace, one of Henry's palaces which still survives. Alternatively children can gain an insight into the grandeur of this palace at www.the-eye.com/hc3.htm.

Ask the children to classify the following activities as those the king would and would not undertake: playing tennis, gambling, buying food, cooking a meal, washing his children, cleaning the palace, meeting ambassadors, listening to music, reading books, writing letters, hunting, playing a musical instrument, signing state papers.

Pages 12 - 13 Henry's pastimes

Ask the children to prepare a display or presentation on Tudor pastimes. Research material from the library, http://www.tudorbritain.org and http://www.historylearningsite.co.uk.

Show pictures or photos of garden mazes. Explain that they were a garden feature favoured by the rich. Let the children draw a design for a maze. A demanding task would be to design a maze using the Logo program. Using the top or base of a box and strips of cardboard, turn the diagram into a model maze. Before pasting each strip to the base, draw a line 1cm from the end, score the line and bend it at right angles. Paste the base of the right angle to the box.

Children can design a Tudor garden at http://www.geffrye-museum.org.uk > Kids' Zone.

The Tudor pastime of real or royal tennis has close associations with Henry VIII. Not only did he play it, but he gambled on it to excess. The site http://www.real-tennis.com explains the game, its rules and its history. This site is for adults with much detailed information on all aspects of the game. Ask children to compare lawn tennis with royal tennis, using a worksheet prepared at their level.

Pages 14 - 15 Henry's problems

Visit the *Mary Rose* site – http://www.maryrose.org – and click on 'Dive in and discover the *Mary Rose*' to take an animated journey. This is a worthwhile exercise which extends the previous work on the website.

Discuss with the children how Princess Mary might have felt about her father's actions and their implications for her future. After the annulment Mary was declared illegitimate and therefore unable to inherit the throne. Henry sent Catherine to a series of rundown castles and houses and forbade Mary from visiting her mother.

Tell the children the story of Thomas More. What does this tell us about Henry as a friend?

Pages 16 - 17 How Henry solved his money problem

The dissolution of the monasteries showed how quickly long-established features of the landscape could be destroyed and altered. The website http://cistercians.shef.ac.uk/ focuses on the five monasteries in Yorkshire with significant standing remains. Although designed for adults, this site has a wealth of material that can be accessed at the children's level. Another useful site is http://www.britainexpress.com/History/medieval-monastery.htm.

Pages 18 -19 Henry and Anne Boleyn

As well as the tour with 'Rascal Raven', there is a more informative tour at http://www.toweroflondontour.com/. Pairs of children could give a short presentation on the tour, using downloaded images.

Pages 20 - 21 Henry and Jane Seymour

Discuss with the children the Tudor attitude to marriage as a means of social betterment.

Let them research the short life of Prince Edward. What sort of schooling did he receive? Did he have any friends? Why was he so attached to his stepmother? How did he get on with his sisters?

Queen Jane died in childbirth and Edward at the age of 14. Encourage the children to research Tudor medicine and suggest reasons why so many children died before adulthood. *Look Inside a Tudor Medicine Chest* by Brian Moses (Hodder Wayland) will provide many answers.

Pages 22 - 23 Henry and Anne of Cleves

After some discussion, set the children the task of writing a letter for Henry, asking Anne of Cleves to marry him. There is some guidance at http://www.tudorbritain.org > Resources.

Share pictures of public figures amongst the children. Ask them to write a description which is accurate but emphasises the person's more pleasing features and ignores their less appealing aspects. Is the person identified when the description is read out to the group?

In pairs, using a digital camera, the children can find out how the camera angle can flatter a subject. They should take five photos of each other. The subject directs the photographer regarding the pose and angle of the shot and selects the 'best' photograph for printing.

Pages 24 - 25 Catherine Howard and Catherine Parr

Each queen took a motto when she married the king. Who had the most suitable motto? Catherine of Aragon: 'Humble and loyal'; Anne Boleyn: 'The most happy'; Jane Seymour: 'Bound to obey and serve'; Anne of Cleves: 'God send me well to keep'; Catherine Howard: 'No other will than his'; Catherine Parr: 'To be useful in all that I do'.

Pages 26 - 27 Six marriages and three children

Give the children a scrambled list of the main events of Henry's reign and ask them to put them in order.

Ask the children for their feelings about Henry. Do they like him? Discuss the important differences between the role of the monarch today and the role of the Tudor monarch.

Following on from discussion of the lists of reasons why Henry married and the reasons why the marriages ended, choose a tune from http://sca.uwaterloo.ca/~praetzel/TOD_2/ and ask the children to write a song, 'The Ballad of Henry VIII'. It should have eight verses: an introduction, one verse for each wife, and their own last verse saying which wife they think did best out of her association with the king.

Local parish churches can be a fruitful source for further investigation. Those built before the Reformation were designed for Catholic ways of worship. Worksheets could be prepared to guide the children around the church and enable them to find and record evidence for the changes in religious practice that took place during the Tudor period.

Index